Poetry lifts the veil from the hidden beauty of the world, and makes familiar objects be as if they were not familiar.

— *Percy Bysshe Shelley*

Also by Greg Stidham:

Propolis for a Fractured World
(Silver Bow Publishing 2024)

Iced Tea Poetry
(Silver Bow Publishing 2023)

Blessings and Sudden Intimacies
(PathBinder Publishers, 2021)

Dear Friends
(PathBinder Publishers, 2021)

Doctoring in Nicaragua
(Finishing Line Press, 2021)

LISTENING TO MILES DAVIS AND GIL EVANS ON A JANUARY NIGHT

poems by

Greg Stidham

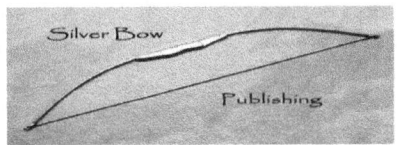

720 Sixth Street, Box # 5
New Westminster, BC
CANADA V3L 3C5

Title: Listening to Miles Davis and Gil Evans on a January Night
Author: Greg Stidham
Cover Art: "Unfinished Symphony" painting by Candice James
Layout and Editing: Candice James
© 2024 Silver Bow Publishing

All rights reserved including the right to reproduce or translate this book or any portions thereof, in any form except for the use of short passages for review purposes, no part of this book may be reproduced, in part or in whole, or transmitted in any form or by any means, electronically or mechanically, including photocopying, recording, or any information or storage retrieval system without prior permission in writing from the publisher or a license from the Canadian Copyright Collective Agency (Access Copyright)
© silver bow publishing
9781774033319 print book
978177403 3326 electronic book

Library and Archives Canada Cataloguing in Publication

Title: Listening to Miles Davis and Gil Evans on a January night / poems by Greg Stidham.
Names: Stidham, Greg, author.
Identifiers: Canadiana (print) 20240516796 | Canadiana (ebook) 20240516818 | ISBN 9781774033319
   (softcover) | ISBN 9781774033326 (Kindle).
Subjects: LCGFT: Poetry.
Classification: LCC PS8637.T535 L57 2024 | DDC C811/.6—dc23

Dedication

To my sons, Chris and Tim, and to my wife, Pam.

Acknowledgment

With many thanks to my editor and publisher and poet, Candice James.

TABLE OF CONTENTS

Nature
Late March Morning / 13
Ladybug / 14
Mating Time / 15
Cardinal / 16
Breakfast / 17
Meditating with Bees / 18
Wild Turkeys in Nebraska / 19
Maysville Heights / 20
Hummingbirds / 21
Landings / 22
November Maple / 23
Inspecting the Hive / 24
November 1 / 25

Sociopolitical
Sirens / 29
Befalling / 30
Toxic Air / 31
Suffering / 32
Afterlife / 34
After-Dinner Headache / 36
Dead Mules in the South / 37

Anecdotes, Moments
Siriusly / 41
Family Photos / 42
Teens / 44
Heavy Snow / 45
Raindrops / 46
Vegan Recipe / 47
Haiku / 48
Challenger / 49
Mount Nebo Sunset / 50
Moon Fade / 51
Beans / 52
The Reading / 53

Grief
Grief Counseling / 57
Confidentiality / 58
Happiness / 59
Bipolar / 60
Colors / 61
Twenty-Sixth Anniversary / 62

Dogs
Love of a Dog / 65
Reactive Dog / 66
Smokey / 67
Holly Wept / 68
Bear / 69
Moment of Calm / 70

Weather
Tornado / 75
Winter's Caprices / 76
Winter Departure / 77
After the Storm / 78
Late Night Storm / 79
Tornado: March, 2023 / 80
Storm / 81
Autumn / 82

Ailments
Poems on Aging / 85
Elk Herd Poems / 86
Déjà Vu / 87
Swollen Feet / 89
Wattle / 90

Personal
Webster Horse / 93
911 / 94
The best time / 95
Birdsongs / 96

Birds / 97
Body Parts / 98
Listening to Miles Davis and Gil Evans on a January Night / 99
Unearthly Conversations / 101
Open Ocean / 102
Heirlooms / 103
Exodus / 104
Rendezvous /105
Self-Pity / 106
Grace / 107
Sweet Rescue / 108
Laments / 109
Flashbacks / 110
Chris / 111
Homecoming / 112
Beards / 113
Spirits in November / 114
The End / 115

NATURE

Late March Morning

The gray squirrel anteloped
on the still-brown grass
below the maple tree
outside my kitchen window.

Gray squirrels are rare in Ontario
where most are jet-black pitch,
but all squirrels have pink inner ears;
gray and black and red alike.

Ladybug

She tip-toes cautiously across the vast green plain,
pausing here, pausing again there, uncertain,
as she feels her wary way ahead.
And then the pause, as she contemplates

her inevitable fate, of fatal fall from the edge,
or incomprehensible annihilation, at the hands
of some god called a human.
She trembles slightly, and the leaf quivers.

Her camouflage spots protected her
from her natural predators — birds,
wasps injecting fertilized eggs into
her armored but still delicate body.

She wanders tremulously to the leaf's edge,
not outdoors, but a plant on the sill
of a sun-brightened kitchen window.

She waits until saved by the gentle brushing
of an enormous finger into
an even more enormous palm,
and released into the morning
outside the kitchen door.

Mating Time

Two great-tailed grackles sat
side by side on a bare
and budless backyard branch,
each plumping feathers
and fanning tails in turn,
one tantalizing the other,

though snow still covers the ground
and snowbanks line the streets,
gray and soiled by auto excrement.

The birds know spring is near,
and the time for making song
and little gracklets not far behind.

Cardinal

A mere foot from the outside
of the cramped bathroom window
were the woven tops of cedars,
frequented in spring
by any number of melodic birds,
close enough to touch
if one could but reach
through the glass unscathed.

Three mornings in a row
a cardinal with its vermillion peak
sat, seeming to peer inside,
a visitor from the past
just checking in.

Breakfast

Over the steam rising above my coffee,
I watch the early-rising chippy
tight-rope across the bannister railing.
He stutter-steps toward the birdfeed,
nestled in a basket hanging from the rail.

The birds have not yet woken,
and the basket is uncommonly calm,
and the chippy, filled with sudden courage
plunges into the inches-deep seed,
scattering it while feasting
before the birds awaken
to forage furiously themselves,
and scatter the seeds
onto the deck,
liberated onto the ground below.

Meditating with Bees

They were busy,
crazy flying from buds
to hive to hide their spoils
in bassinette cells scrubbed clean
for new nectar, and new pollen,
before honey for new babies,
eggs laid 3000 a day
by the intrepid queen.

They were so busy,
frenetic, coming and going,
but their buzz mesmerizing,
lulling a novice beekeeper
into a trance of sorts,
hearing the almost
unchanging timbre and timing.

And for an hour he sat,
hypnotized into a meditative trance;
and felt, at last,
part of something
bigger than himself.

Wild Turkeys in Nebraska

At a rest stop in Nebraska,
a long day's drive at a welcome end,
we watch others come and go.

A couple with two
young children in tow,
like the car they pull
behind their pickup.

A woman in too-warm sweats
pulls off and exits her car,
cell phone camera in hand,
begins photographing
to the southeast where there is
nothing but cornfields, until we spy
the rainbow high in the sky
above dark clouds
where distant lightning flickers.

We're near where
Sandhill Cranes pause
to refresh along the Platte River
on their thousand-mile migration to Canada.

Though, tonight, the only birds
speckling the fields
are wild turkeys.

Maysville Heights

On this barren mesa,
at 8400 feet,
winds roar in
from the Divide just west.

They strip opening car doors
from the hands of drivers,
and make sober men
stumble down wooden stairs.

They force the rugged piñons
to grow aslant, stirring dust
between them and
wild sagebrush.

The mountains shade dusk's light
still spilling from their peaks
to the darkening valleys below.

And when the winds have calmed
and the night's dark is lit
by stars and a near-full moon,
a herd of thirty or more elk
saunter, unperturbed,
a hundred feet from our log home
and the warmth of a strong blaze
in its hearth.

Hummingbirds

They come up the valley from the south;
their annual migration north.
We are at a stopover, a rest stop,
a restaurant with late April/early May
wildflower blossoms
in hanging clay pots
beckoning seductively.

You can hear the birds
without seeing them,
buzzing harshly like electricity
fizzing along high voltage wires
from a burning-out transformer.

For all their noise, you're
lucky to see them
as they hover motionless
before the colorful petals,
their wings invisible.

In an instant
as short as the one
when they appeared,
the electric buzzing
is replaced by total silence.

Landings

Maple tree helicopter seeds
spiral down, littering the side patio,
layers thickening on the patio table
like large snowflakes in December,
until a gust of wind exhaled by the lake
lifts them as one and scatters them
about the patio stones.

Midnight confetti
on New Year's Eve.

November Maple

Just two days into November
and the maple tree stands
stripped of all but a few handfuls
of brown and yellow
and yellow-green leaves,
looking like
a frail octogenarian
nearly naked,
before bed.

Inspecting the Hive

Two stories tall, this
apartment building is safe,
the queen and brood mostly
on the first floor,
the workers preparing the second
for a future move-in, preparing
nesting rooms, cleaning,
readying for honey
and then an egg,
making room
for the next generation.

November 1

Stripped now of the last
of the small red leaves,
the grey dogwoods
stand straight
with spindly fingers
like those on the hand
of a skeleton arm
planted upright,
like a decoration
on this day after Halloween.

SOCIOPOLITICAL

Sirens

The sirens sound but with a different timbre,
softer than the primal wail of an hour ago,
when the skies turned yellow,
and the wind calmed to utter stillness.
And thoughts turned to Dorothy
and Toto, and the yellow brick road,
and the razed town of Rolling Fork,
Mississippi, just down the road.

Halfway around the world sirens
just like these signal
incoming volleys of missiles
and elders and children,
and parents have nowhere to hide,

like I do not, with my wife,
my two beloved dogs who trust me,
no where to turn or hide
as the vacuum gale sucks us up,
or the explosion engulfs us
before we can even think to pray.

Befalling

Night falls early
on the eastern side
of the mountains...

But *befalls*? What befalls, but
tragedy: *tragedy befalls
us innocent bystanders.*

The early falling of sunset,
beyond the still-snowcapped
mountains to the west,
makes dusk descend earlier.

But no homes implode,
no children are buried,
like places where elders awake
and grieve, where
the unimaginable has befallen.

Dawn compensates
when dusk descends early,
by rising even earlier,
giving breath to newfound
optimism,

while the grievers dig,
with blunt shovels,
shallow graves
to rest their children,
with barren white crosses

marking where their
parents can find them
in some other time.

Toxic Air

The searing sun
burns its way through
the thick orange haze hanging,
shroud-like, over the city's skyline;
the stifling fog migrated down
from the wildfires up north,
so remote they are unreachable
by fearless firefighters,
but intimate with
my burning throat.

Suffering

this world may be short on ozone,
water too in some places, even food,
but suffering and pain
are in endless supply

innocent men, women, children
slaughtered in the desert
where both sides suffer
a dearth of morality

a grandmother pulled over
for a bogus traffic stop
shot and killed for doing
nothing

a young woman on the phone today
grieving the suicide loss
of her step-father,
the only father she's known

and an elderly mother's
ear-splitting wailing
months after
the loss of her daughter

suffering accumulates
like refuse in a landfill

a manure pile
piled beside the barn
small profits when sold

or putrid, fly-infested,
disgusting when not

how to replenish ozone
before it's too late

how to scoop the landfill
into recycling

how to calm the wails
of the mourning mother

touch on her outstretched
forearm, another binge
of frustrated silence

how to listen
to the pain
of the woman
whose father killed
himself   not
worrying that
his daughter
is in knots
and crying

Afterlife

My father, whom I scarcely knew,
still lives in the afterlife, like
the woman I thought I loved
who cashed in her own ticket.

We all know someone there,
in the afterlife, in that someplace
where souls go when they go,
where they live on.

And we know this
because we feel it, we
feel them, we talk to them,
and sometimes they talk back

from this afterlife; after all,
we were taught about it as children.
We were taught about how
part of it is good and pleasant,

fun, and we dreamed of ice cream cones
and chocolate cake, no belly aches.
But if we sinned, if we stole
or lied or yelled at our mom,

the afterlife was not so good,
and they taught us about the fires
of hell, and red-skinned
pitchforked monsters, with long barbed tails.

And still we believe in this afterlife.
We talk to passed-on spouses,
or parents or lovers, we
even ask them for protection.

But what if this afterlife lives
only in our imaginations, and
the voices of our spouses, lovers
likewise—our imaginations.

What if the afterlife exists only
in the neurons of our hippocampus,
where other memories also reside,
waiting to be brought to life?

What if the afterlife lives
as long as our hippocampus does,
as long as we pump our blood,
our oxygen to its fragile cells,

then it will keep them healthy,
those fussy neurons,
and then I can call on them,
and I can see my father

flying a model airplane,
my grandfather throwing
a head-spinning curveball,
and I can see my lover

flash her fingers shaped like a heart,
remember Jessica who never made two,
they will all live as long as I do,
me and my happy
hippocampus neurons.

After-Dinner Headache

After dinner tonight I held
my head in my hands, and rubbed
my temples, soothing a headache
before its full arrival,

and then I felt a ridge
above my left temple,
not matched on my right,
and I thought how odd,
and, pondering, forgot
my incoming headache.

Instead I thought of pictures
of Cro-Magnon skulls
and Neanderthals, and I wondered,
did they have headaches too?
And wondered too about these
human cousins, how they comingled,
if at all,

before realizing
my impending headache
was in full retreat.

Dead Mules in the South
A dead mule is something you can't ignore.
It makes its way metaphorically and has to make a point.
  ~ Jerry Mills, Professor of English, University of North Carolina.

I am an animal lover/sucker.
Animal rescues drain my money.
Most are dog rescues, but some
are broader, and bigger—
farm animal rescues,
or organizations saving
horses from human abuse,
and occasionally a plea comes
from a rescue seeking to save
donkeys from their daily
debilitating beatings,
or slaughter for food and skin.

But no one pleads the case
or begs for funds
for the rescue of mules,
the misfit offspring,
the half-breeds, the
Métis of the equine world.

Sterile, they are no threat
to any herder, any hoarder
who sees nothing beyond
their value as laborers,
or cheap food for men
or other animals.

Gentle and kind, they only
wish for and never get the same.
They get worked to death.
They get driven in numbers
over cliffs in the Southwest.
They get slaughtered,
eaten once they've served
their duty carrying heavy packs

over narrow mountain trails;
or pulling ploughs through
rough Alabama clay.

When they're done,
they're done.
Their time is done,
and slaughter is
their long-sought release,
in fiction or southern farmlands,
behind closed doors of predawn dark,
or after-bedtime
rifle shots in the night.

ANECDOTES, MOMENTS

Siriusly

She says to Siri,
"Show me men's names
that begin with C."
And with dutiful technology
Siri responds,
"I found this on the web."

She wants to know this
because she has
forgotten the name
of a neighbor's dog,
and feels certain
it begins with a C.

"Carson!" she exclaims,
after scrolling through
a dozen or so names,
relieved that
her memory's lapse
will not keep her
awake tonight.

But then she says,
"His name is Carson,
and the dog is Storm."

And I realize
she got it all wrong,
the name of the dog
and the name of the owner,
which I do all the time,
but she'll be sleeping tonight
just fine, thanks to Siri.

Family Photos

Crowding the surface of the fold-up table,
long as an aircraft carrier,
was most everything you could want,
if you were patient and searched carefully.

Electric mixer from the 60s, one blender missing.
A child's wind-up model car,
      a green '69 Mustang.
An antique hair curling iron
      that could have passed
          for 19th century medical forceps.
A hand-cranked drill with a handful of bits.

And at the end of the stable sits
a short stack of photographs, portraits,
in ornate metal frames, all bearing proudly
the patina of age, stacked
carelessly in two or three piles:

The matronly beyond-middle-aged woman,
grandmother perhaps, gray hair piled
in the discreet mound of a bun,
her blouse with high collar
buttoned tight at her neck.

Two newlyweds on a honeymoon
at a gray-sandy beach,
her swim attire in two chaste pieces,
his like the costume of a boxer in the ring
before gloves were used,
the waves in the background
smoothed by the camera's blur.

A young father sitting, legs
folded beneath, as if in prayer
before the circular train track,
a 5-year-old boy beside,
the monochrome Christmas tree behind.

A closet cleaned out by someone
is now nearly barren of things,
and the browsing man also
barren of ideas
of who these people are,
now for sale
for a quarter or two.

Teens

Four drives down they sat,
legs outstretched
facing each other
on their skateboards,
rolling slightly to and fro,
talking seriously
at fourteen or fifteen.

And then they were gone,
each I imagined back home
to parents and dinner,
siblings and homework,
but not without a certain glow.

Heavy Snow

With the pinkie side of her balled up fist
she wiped circles in the frosted kitchen window,
and opened a portal to the snow falling outside.

They were large flakes, wet and heavy,
and the mounting layers were heavy too.

Shoveling would be near impossible,
and snow blowers crippled by the weight.

It was snow like this,
earlier this year,
that took her shoveling neighbor,
kindly, portly, white-haired and wise,
when she, at ten, was just learning
to spread her butterfly wings.

Raindrops

The sound of raindrops
tapping bashfully
on rooftop and walls,
a romantic scene
in a wood cabin
high in the Rockies.

But there is no rain,
no sign of rain but for
the raindrop sound,
made by the softly bubbling
humidifier nearly empty of water.

Vegan Recipe

Tofu, soft tofu, into the blender,
and add all kinds of spices,
fresh or dried, it doesn't matter,
blend it into a dip-like sauce
and give it a taste—
if it needs something, a little kick,
add some hot chili flakes,
then blend it till it's smooth,
and scoop it into a small dish,
line the dish with baby carrots
and splintered broccoli stems,
and enjoy an appetizer
that didn't kill any creature
that once had a mother.

Haiku

The origami sailboat
tip-toes on still glass
mountain pond water

Challenger

Billowing smoke, fire like sun,
a glorious beginning.
Five crew—four men and a woman,
the first teacher in space, her students

and others around the world watching.
Televisions flickered in classrooms,
excited children transfixed, mission control
counting backwards to ignition and liftoff.

The rocket rose, seemed to stand still,
then accelerated spaceward until
seventy-nine seconds later
the explosion,

and humans
freefalling 50,000 feet.

Mount Nebo Sunset

Sitting on the grass
sloping toward the precipice
on the west face of Mount Nebo,
a small group gathers

to watch the sun setting, the brilliant
orange orb descending against
the unbesmirched blue sky,
and if you watch carefully enough

you can see the slow movement
as the sun's lower lip narrows the gap
to the level line of the distant horizon.
Soon the sun is sitting on the earth,

its bottom now shaved to a short
flat edge, as the backdrop drape of sky
turns deeper blue
and the sun's dropping

is measured in minutes.
In two it hides entirely
beneath the earth,
and the people rising

from their beach towels and blankets,
begin to disperse. Already
the sky is star-freckled,
and flashlights light the path
      back up the slope.

Moon Fade

The nearly full moon was not stark,
but tempered, filtered.

There were no moon shadows,
but an ambience, a calming
romantic glow.

It lasted some twenty
delicious minutes before
clouds began to drift in
slowly obscuring
the moon's margins.

The night grew darker,
like most nights, and
the ambient romantic glow
faded into coal-colored sky,
now devoid even of stars,

until all was overcast,
and dark, and my communion
with the ambient moonlight
devolved into darkness,
and aloneness once again
cast its shawl over me.

Beans

The vines reach up
hand over hand
grappling a lolling
string hanging from
a crossbeam in the garden,
looping their tendrils
around the string,
pulling themselves up,
marines in boot camp,
up toward their siblings.

In another few weeks,
they'll be so tall
I might just see
Jack climbing up,
taking care not to fall.

The Reading

The bulbous boy
stood before the microphone,
eyes wide and white,
the papers in his hand shaking
almost imperceptibly.

His chubby jowls
made him look
more a child
than the pubescent
young man he was.

He cleared his throat nervously,
his voice cracking
as he began to read
his first poem.

GRIEF

Grief Counseling

The weight of the dialog
dragged me down
as I walked through the kitchen door.
The pain of the client,
as he railed in anguish
that he painted in words
after his wife and one son
perished in the fiery crash.
The echoes of his words
pulled on my feet like
heavy sucking mud.

Confidentiality

I tell her bits and pieces of their stories,
but not their names or other
identifying information, their stories
too personal, too horrific.

She can hear my side
of the phone counseling
conversations, and sometimes
the muffled voices
during Zoom support groups,
    and

it affects her, makes her teary,
and somehow she shares with me
my sadness, my stress,
my sense of powerlessness.

Happiness

So many times I have asked
the question and received no answer.
The intimidating "why?"
And why, when I swore
I would not be scarred,
have I been so crippled?

The dreams have become sparse,
once weekly or biweekly,
now two or three times a year,
cherished when they visit.

Haunted, but not scarred?
I try to fool myself,
but I remain baffled
by the *why*?

And then the rare dream:
memory of running
into Memphis downpour
from opposite directions
to meet at the corner,
with marble sidewalk
slick as snail snot, we ran
toward each other
for thirty seconds of connection
embraced, maybe kissed,
turned and ran back
in opposite directions.

But I slipped on the slick marble,
banged my head silly,
yet I was happy.
For the first time in decades,
I was happy.

Bipolar

It's that time again, time
for depression, time
to leave the kids with grandma.
It's time to take two
litre-bottles of vodka
and your father's vintage
shotgun, in the old
nearly antique caddy.
Time to drive off to the woods
nobody visits and find
a campsite that won't see a tent
or a campfire, besides the one
that rages in your soul.

Colors

A word comes
from nowhere
a word
violaceous
as though
from a dream
violaceous
a fruit
a bruise
a tender rash
the sky
    at sunset
the sky
    before sunrise
the transition
    from good mood
    to less good
memories of one
    possibly bipolar
and the stain
    on her white night
    gown
violaceous

Twenty-Sixth Anniversary

The thick orange haze hangs
over the city's skyline
like an otherworldly shroud
the searing sun cannot penetrate;
but it heats the strangling air below
to record high temperatures.

Am I in hell?

DOGS

Love of a Dog

The nose scarcely felt
by my fingers hanging
over the side of my bed,
unrecognized, unnoticed
in my sleep until
his wet nose nudges
more assertively,
and his punk hair-do
pushes against my hand.

Before my alarm sounds
I am aware
morning has arrived,

and the rescue dog
with PTSD wants connection,
reassurance that—what?
I am alive?
That I still love him?
That I'll still pet his
curly facial fur
at 6 a.m.?

I moan and turn.
Yes, I will.

Reactive Dog

Two dogs,
one twelve years perhaps,
losing control of his bowels,
at night his bladder too.

He has always been Zen,
and we called him our Zen-dog,
who'd never met a dog
or a human he didn't like,
who tolerated frenetic abuse
from excited puppies without a flinch,
who faced reactive aggressive curs
with mere curiosity
before walking away non-plussed.

The other was young,
a refugee from a war-zone
in the streets of Beirut,
come to us with PTSD,
reactive to loud noises, large humans,
to skate-boarding teens,
to my grandson who loomed,
parka and hoodie-adorned
as he tried to lean over
to pet him the first time,
only to get nipped.

But don't we all have
our peculiar backgrounds
that make us sometimes passive,
or others that make us
fearful, and reactive in ways
that seem aggressive?

Smokey

He slipped to his side on the hardwood floor,
exhausted after an afternoon of seizures,
and I curled behind him, like a lover spooning,
though he didn't notice.

I spooned the giant Shepherd,
until we both fell asleep
awakening surprised in the morning,
both still breathing:
it was not quite his time just yet.

My arm draped over his fur,
his calm body softly breathing,
and I wanted him not to go,
though if he must, I thought,
perhaps I should too,
a thought quickly squelched
for an excess of melodrama.

Holly Wept

Driving across the flat high plains
of western Nebraska, northeastern
Colorado, dry dirt and cornfields,
following signs to Fort Morgan,

where Dexter our dog lived
for half a year in the
Humane Society Shelter,
waiting for his forever family.

He was the special dog, the favorite
of all the staff, who made him
the "greeter," keeping him in front,
at the foot of the reception desk.

They were sad and happy
when we adopted him, and
they waved, wishing him
and us well as we drove off.

Six years later we
retrace the route
stopping at the shelter
for the staff to see their greeter,

now old and infirm, but still
the gentlest dog we've ever known.
He and they
deserve this reunion.

Holly saw him struggle in,
and together they collapsed on the floor.
She stroked him and spoke softly,
leaning over to enwrap his neck.

She buried her face in his fur,
and her shoulders
began to bob, and
we heard her deep breaths.

Bear

We call him Bear.
A rescue dog from Beirut,
he has PTSD and he snaps
unpredictably at occasional dogs,
and rarely at people.

But at home he craves touches
and affection, and is
brother and protector
to his 14-year-old ailing housemate,
our other rescue, his soulmate.

Moment of Calm

Dexter, the dog,
fourteen or more years old,
lies quietly at my feet,
not anxious,
not breathing fast,
but calm.

Not like this often,
he works hard
to arrive at this state.
He paces round
the circumscribed kitchen,
in circles.

He sips water this turn around,
and then sips a bit more the next.
Each time he passes where I sit,
I reach to pat his head,
to scratch his back,
to ruffle his jowls
and his turkey neck.

At last he lies down,
a tormented dog whose torment
has somehow lessened,
at least for now.

Near-paralyzed hind legs,
unable to control his bladder
or his bowels, he struggles
every minute of every day,
his days limited,
confused, frustrated,
and embarrassed.

This moment of calm,
while he seems to sleep or
at least to rest, quietly,

fills my heart with helium
and lifts it like a balloon
into the depths of the night sky,
so infinite, with so much room
for this spiritually advanced dog.

WEATHER

Tornado

First, grey clouds fade darkly
into black while winds whip up
and air turns tomb-like cold.
Raindrops the size of marbles

smack the windshield and rooftop
like a drumstick on a tight snare drum,
while the sun retreats to safer chambers,
and people feel the first pangs of fear.

Then, in the mirror, the funnel of smoke,
the vortex sucking cars and homes.
Fear becomes panic   fleeing
crazy driving and pandemonium.

Winter's Caprices

Three days ago snow banks five feet tall
hid children scuffing on sidewalk ice
home from school, parents half hidden as well.

And today the sun glares from a cloudless sky
and the banks are shrinking, the sidewalks and street
nearly dry, children pass on iceless concrete.

In six months, this road
will exhale traces of
summer steam after rain
under a sun glaring like today.

Winter Departure

Raindrops from dark gray skies slosh
into puddles surrounding like moats
cadavers of the melting snowbanks
soiled now with aged salt
and automobile excrement.

Though well above freezing
the air feels colder, more bitter
than during snowstorms
just weeks ago.

Moods are gray too,
passersby tuck chins
into coat collars or
the occasional scarf,
eyes cast down, no
chance for hello,
or a friendly glance of eye.

March is near,
but this is how
winter chooses departure.

After the Storm

Birds sing,
the sky is blue,
white clouds slip by,
the lights are back on,
blackness now gone,
the hailstones too,
the fierce winds lashing,
rattling windows,
the flashing of lightning,
detonations of thunder,
the tornado that touched down
thirty miles east.

They are all gone,
the wind now
a contrite and gentle
breeze, a coolness
brushing the cheek
awakes to a new world.

Late Night Storm

The rain came as they said it would,
after midnight, 2 a.m.
and the humid breeze
stilled to sudden silence,
minutes before the flash
announced the arrival
of curtain sheets of unleashed rain,
now lashed by wailing wind.

The sound on the side of the house
was like the steady static
of haybale-sized brushes
of the street cleaners in spring.

In ten minutes
the rain stopped
as suddenly as it started,
and the night fell,
once again, silent.

Tornado: March, 2023

Surfing over asphalt
on Highway 55
in northeast Arkansas,
watching white-knuckled
the black curtains drape
over white afternoon
April sun, and darkness
settled like the dusk
of 3 p.m. Gethsemane,
while the winds
redoubled their assault.

Peanut-sized raindrops
pelted the windshield,
while wipers on high
flailed futilely against
the relentless rain.

In a small town
a few miles off the highway,
Thor unleashed his
ugly black finger
from sky to ground
leveling buildings and
killing helpless cattle.

Storm

Winds whipped through tall trees,
ripping down branches beneath a black
and lightless sky while
the sound of hail
pounding the trailer's roof
echoed within, the sky
blazing white with lightning
casting tree shadows
on briefly lit ground.

Autumn

It's that time again,
the time of cool mornings,
dewdrops dotting windshields,
the trees blushing and unfastening
their crimson and amber,
dropping them coyly
to the stubbled lawn.

The time of cool mornings
demanding the use of sleeves:
hoodies, flannel shirts,
only to be shed by midafternoon,
like leaves cast aside and strewn
beside the rumpled bed.

AILMENTS

Poems on Aging

I am exhausted by poems
bemoaning ailments
accompanying aging,

especially my own.
Enough is enough.
The ailments never improve.

Attitudes are not uplifted.
They certainly won't uplift
the unknown reader who

suffers similarly
achy knees, poor balance,
even peeing in Morse code.

Elk Herd Poems

What writer at seventy-two
immortalizing the flesh sagging
from his upper arms,
like a turkey's wattle
that wobbles slightly
when the arm is raised
to greet a passing neighbor,
has not also written at fifty
about foibles like
a bad knee, or a beer belly
he just noticed for the first time.

    I prefer poems,
about a herd of elk passing
along a mountain mesa at dusk,
on their way to drinking water,
    to poems whining about
irrepressible thoughts of mortality.

Déjà Vu

The first time I wasn't sure
what my body was saying to me.
A slightly upset belly and a pain,
below my ribs on the left,
and howls like animals in pain,
not hunger grumbles,
or thunder forewarning
a dysenteric eruption.
They were sounds not familiar,
with a faint echo, until
the symptoms abated
and I dismissed them,
some anomaly, something I ate.

Days later they were back
in force, accompanied this time
by stomach swelling,
and when I tapped my belly
the sound was that
of a tightly stretched drum head,

all leading to surgery, and removal
of a length of sigmoid colon...

No, not cancer, and I was free
to live another eight years
with nothing but common
digestive complaints.

This time is different. No.
It is the same, the same vague
discomfort, the same loud, tympanic
echoes from the same
upper left quadrant,

with a low-grade fever.
It's not the same but damn near.

In my mind I've written this poem
        from fear.
My body is eight years older than then
and I question whether it can survive
        another surgery.
And I've thought of colostomy bags,
and how can my wife
whom I love beyond belief
ever make love with me,
        with my bag between us.

And I've thought of slipping out,
while under anesthesia—no pain,
no awareness,

but what about
all the stuff on my computer,
password-protected,
bank accounts, pension plans,
social security,
and I worry about compiling
a list of those passwords,
and locating them somewhere
my wife can find them,
so her work may somehow
be lessened.

Swollen Feet

Sandal straps too short
to straddle my swollen feet.
I am embarrassed
to wear them out,
to be seen with ankles
thick as hams,
toes like sausages.

These feet are not for walking,
and I just want to take them
with me to bed
and let them lie,
unperturbed in the pocket
of the tucked-in sheet
at the bottom of the bed,
where they can listen to me
moan and whine.

Wattle

I imagine the upper arms
of my two adult sons,
toned, biceps defined,
triceps too, I wonder…
will they feel how I did
when I first noticed
the waggle of loose skin
beneath my own,
like the wattle
below a turkey's neck.

PERSONAL

Webster Horse

His belly was torn,
his eyes were missing.
His mane was made
of shaggy strands of yarn.

His name was Webster Horse,
and he shared a bed with my son.
He came with him
to doctors' appointments,
even to church,

hardly ever leaving his arms
until the girl got sick,
seriously sick,
and he gave her
his best friend,
Webster Horse.

911

His body was folded
on the sticky floor
like a pocket knife
opened halfway,
his flannel pajama bottoms
below his buttocks,
the hardwood soiled.

He was confused, said he'd
fallen three times, couldn't get up.
He lived alone.
No one could reach him
all afternoon.

The paramedics helped
raise him to his feet,
helped to clean him
and helped with clean pants.

They gently lifted him
onto the gurney and
into the back of their vehicle,
then took him from his house
to Emergency.

The best time

to feel your
fingers grazing
the skin of my shoulder
is in the morning
before the sun comes up
before the clamor
of the trucks
in search of garbage,
before the commotion
of me getting up to pee.

That is the best time
to feel your touch
your fingers on the bare skin
of my shoulder beneath
the sheet and the covers
to know that you too
feel the need to connect
if only with a finger
before the start
of the rigors of the day

Birdsongs

Oh, chickadee, take your black cap
and your sweet and happy song,
take it somewhere else,
and take your goldfinch with you
and her joyful trill,
somewhere far away.

My mood is too dark today
to be swayed by your allure.

Take as well your robin friend's
assertiveness, he gives little
and takes nothing.

Or even your blue jay cousin,
with his pretty chirp's
flirty deceptions.

Just leave me alone
with your distant cousin
mourning dove,

and together we can
mourn this world
fractured beyond repair.

Birds

A plastic model
of a Baltimore Oriole,
plastic pieces pieced
together and glued
just like the models
of the P-38 Lightning,
or the F-4U Corsair,
a 6-year old's fascination
with World War II's warbirds
suddenly startled
by a grandfather's gift—
a model of a stalwart bird,
but not a fighter,
who sees his fledglings,
his eggs, even his spouse,
fall prey to lesser birds.

Body Parts

These arms were never specimens,
never arms of a weightlifter, though
they served me well enough
when I was young, and after.

They embraced my father's shoulders,
as they wheeled his gurney away,
his weak arms embracing me back,
that last time we spoke.

These legs were once trim and solid,
runner's legs, before strange
chronic illness weakened them,
and standing steady was but a memory.

These legs helped me lift
my father's flaccid body
to help carry him to the car,
the 200-mile drive to a _real_ hospital.

The six-pack abdomen never happened,
but I fist-punched it with pride
in front of my sons, then a memory
of the photo of my father fresh

out of the navy standing
sun-drenched on a beach,
arms raised and flexed
like an Atlas impersonator.

Both overweight and shriveled now
I try to remember those years
when youth ran unrestrained,
like his did after the war.

The last time we spoke,
as the gurney gathered speed
out the door and down the hall,
we exchanged whispered _I love you_'s.

Listening to Miles Davis and Gil Evans on a January Night

The scents of garlic
and strong black pepper
drift from the pan
of thick split pea soup
to my eager nostrils,
and more garlic aroma,
as the buttered and
spiced bread toasts.

Outside darkness is undisturbed
by moon or stars, cold enough
to cause piss-shivers.
No cars pass
this neighborhood road,
no bikers, runners,
walkers with or without
their head-lighted dogs.

When it's time to serve,
I do my part,
and play music
on my diminutive speaker,
fed by phone and Bluetooth,
Sketches of Spain.

The mournful strains of the Adagio
evoke some Andalusian pain,
and we blow on the spoonful
of tongue-scalding soup,
then relish the spicy
baked samosas on the side,
and with lights dimmed,
conversation silenced by the cold,
dark outdoors and the solemnity
of Miles' careful solos, the trombone
of an unknown brass player.

We sip the soup, and the red wine,
and list into separate reveries,
into separate worlds ...
together.

Unearthly Conversation

The elderly man, white-bearded,
with balding pate, and black cane in hand,
spoke softly enough.

*Don't act quickly or without careful thought
about the first woman you ask to marry.
Know her first, not just well,
but well enough to know her fears,
her demons. Learn about her family
and their demons as well.*

*Wait until your late twenties, do not
assume you know as much as needed,
or can know now and learn much more.*

*Do not ignore, or rationalize behaviors
that seem odd or different,
however benign they seem.
Be wary, learn more. Take more years.*

The younger man, clean-shaven,
curly locks cascading past his ears,
listened politely, but dismissively,
knowing what he knew, knowing
that he loved this woman, accepted
her imperfections and vowed to stand
behind her, to help her grow,
to help her vanquish her demons,
whatever they were.

He did not listen, did not follow
any implied offers of advice,
following instead his meager
and myopic juvenile vision.

Open Ocean

Settle your hull
into the sea of my soul,
feel your buoyancy
lifted up by the rise
and swell of me.

Feel safe and unsinkable,
even when winds
become tempestuous:
they do not last.

Lie with me
until the rhythms quell,
until my breathing slows
and stills, and I will
send you off
with gentle breeze
and sadness,
but grateful
to have known you.

Heirlooms

He sat in this chair,
this square-backed comfort chair
with matching ottoman,
my grandfather, when
the chair was new,
in the late 40's.

It was a decade old
when I first met it,
my grandfather slouching,
watching baseball
on a black-and-white
television, but listening
to the radio announcers
he thought were better,
feet propped up.

He died in that chair,
in his sleep, after
the stroke, and the
painful rehab.

That chair
reupholstered sits
in my cluttered office
separated from the ottoman
downstairs, barely used.

When I glance at that chair
I see my grandfather,
winding up and hurling
a sweeping curveball
at Louisville Colonels' stadium,
and a sweeping strike and miss,
the last out.

Exodus

Muscles tensed in grimace,
perhaps pain, perhaps fear,
relaxed,

as I walked through the door,
and the outline of a smile
traced his face,
sapping the only energy left
from the grimace,
and his body's tension
relaxed,
he leaned back
into his two pillows.

He was glad to see me
I could see,
and I wanted to weep.
I'd come to recover him
from small town Arkansas,
carry him to the big city,
where the reason would be found
that his legs no longer held him,
the reason he shook
like leaves in a tropical storm,
his soul lashed by the stings
of brutal rainfall.

With help, my son and I
carried him to our van,
then began the trip home,
home ... being the hospital
where he'd spend
his final days.

Forty years later I feel tears
that only ambush on rare occasion,
like when I've sat,
trying to write.

Rendezvous

1.

Two orange orbs
skin-peeled before me.
Each wedge bursts
with startling sweetness.

2.

A juvenile male redbird
alights on a still-bare branch,
and stares through my window,
watching, watching,
then joined by his mate,
lifts up and away.

3.

An entire afterlife
exists, vibrant here,
in the center of my brain.

Self-Pity

For two years I've watched
the self-pity leak like
oil from a car
onto the white driveway,
drip, drip, and I wait
for the leak to seal,
or the reservoir to run dry.

But there seems no end,
and the sweet-sour smell
of self-pity taints
those watching from afar,
drip, drip.

Grace

My grand-daughter's name is Grace,
which makes me think
of the blessing prayer
before meals, makes me think
of grace and blessings
offered by bible thumpers
in the deep south.

Tonight Grace video-called,
eyes red, nose sniffling,
wanting to talk,
and only Grandpa would do.

Sweet Rescue

Syrupy sweet swallows of Apera
sliding past my palate
rescue me from distasteful
thoughts dredged from past pain.

Present pain is less easily assuaged.
The clot needs to congeal
and the bleeding staunched,
before the pain begins to remit.

Laments

Strains of Ralph Vaughn Williams
stir my soul, but fail to quell
the disquiet I feel,
which I don't understand,

this unsettledness, this
barrage of memories,
none linked but all powerful
and I don't try to wrestle them.

Like dreams they return,
the missed opportunities,
relationships that never really were
what they could have been.

This poem is not tasteful,
just like all the others
that lament pasts
unrecoverable,

leaving me wondering
if laments mean anything.

Flashbacks
(for Larry G.)

We are talking about plumbing
in a rental house we own in Memphis,
where Larry lived,

and another rental where
an absolutely naïve renter
is stymied by a leaky
kitchen faucet.

So we called a plumber
who was also Larry's in-law,
and we had to call him again
for help in another house,

and like the heat-wave vision
of low blood pressure,
a wave of sadness
poured over my soul.

Chris

He had chronic kidney failure
        dialysis
          three times a week

Wheel-chair bound
        meeting friends for lunch
        a challenge

Face never missing a smile
        he refused the help
        of a wheelchair push

Once an athlete of near-Olympic ability
        now shamed by his chair
        his curved spine

The spine was never broken
        until his marriage failed
        his will began to fade

My infrequent emails became
        frequently unanswered
        until no answers at all

Guilty I fell silent until
        curious, I Googled
        and found his obituary

Homecoming

it feels so good
to be home again
to hear your
unspoken voice
to listen to your
soundless whispers
your breathiness
to lay my head
in the lap
of your gentle waves
and to answer
quietly
speaking in tongues

Beards

My beard was at its best when it was bushy,
long enough to land mid-chest dripping
after a shower. Not complicated,
it was white and sprouting
out from cheeks like the jowls
of a large chipmunk, white enough
to make me mistaken for Santa Claus,
especially in December.

Others thought it too unruly,
made me look like a madman,
William Blake persona perhaps,
unsettling at least,
and so I succumbed:

I trimmed, and I hated
my tidy trimmed look,

and I swore
I'd never trim again.

Spirits in November

The bone-chill of a November night,
temperature just barely freezing,
but it's still so wet
bones feel frozen
and fingers cold,
without sensation.

Outside it is black,
no stars punching through
whatever clouds I can't even see.
A streetlight floods the street
with white light as sterile
as light in an operating room,
and nothing seems real
as it does during the day.

Spirits drift unseen
in the dark tonight,
their faint whispers
the only sign
of their presence.

The End

My manuscript, first full
collection of poems
trolls empty waters
in search of a publisher,
and I am disappointed and frustrated
until I realize that it does not matter,
just like Everything
does not matter.

We are all together
on a dirgeful procession
toward the unavoidable
cliff of extinction, along with
all our other fellow humans
of all races, and all other animals
of all species, and plants
and even microbes alike.

There is no God who will
turn his back on his relentless wrath
and in a moment of reconsideration
become compassionate
and save us from our fate.

There is no God, no gods
but those we have created
with our imaginations
to help us answer the unanswerable—
the meaning, the purpose
of our existence.
Like our gods, our meaning and purpose
are creatures of our imagination,
that give us the temporary illusion
of some comfort.

There are no gods but those
of our own creation, whose whims
we've followed for eons

to justify our slaughter
of fellow humans.

We are on the path to extinction
at the hand of our planet
which is destroying us just
as we have destroyed it,
never imagining a solar oven
baking us to non-existence,
or a toxic and
unbreathable atmosphere
and poisoned waters, of floods
greater than those imagined
by the writers of our God's history,
and droughts that parch
once-fertile fields of grain.

We have mostly failed to imagine
our own insignificance,
but for a few who saw us,
our planet, our solar system,
our galaxy as tiny
specks of irrelevance,
here one nanosecond, gone the next,
with no cosmic entity to mourn us,
to take note of our passing,
as there has been none to notice
our trivial existence.

In two or three generations,
all that we have known will cease,
green forests and grassy fields
becoming hard baked rock
of minerals. Water,
water that created us
will disappear, the skyscrapers,
those monuments to our greed
and overindulgence,
will collapse upon themselves.

My poems,
virgins to the ears of readers
will fall over the cliff of extinction,
like all art—literature, music, theater,
cinema—all in the good company
of us humans and all life as we know it,
following our forebears—dodo,
wooly mammoth, clouded leopard, laughing owl—
all over the edge.

I will say goodbye to my poems,
goodbye to my loving spouse,
goodbye to a few friends
accrued through several decades,
goodbye to memories of parents,
first girlfriends, first-born and
second-born sons,
goodbye to music I have loved,
goodbye to parts of this planet
I have loved in their
heartbreakingly beautiful splendor,

and say hello
to the nearly unimaginable,
say hello to the "what's next,"
hello to   nothing.

www.ingramcontent.com/pod-product-compliance
Lightning Source LLC
Chambersburg PA
CBHW052148070526
44585CB00017B/2024